M

# MY HEART TO HEART WITH LOVE – GOD 2021

In order for Demons to get you to Sin, and you solidifying your place in hell, they have to; must get you to sin by you going against the Law and Laws of Life.

Thus, the different Bibles of Men that billions of you believe in and trust.

Your Political Leaders that get you to Sin day in and day out with their different Laws that are truly unjust.

Your Political Leaders that send you on the Battlefield of Death to die. Thus, you breaking the "thou shalt not kill" law.

Your Religious Lies that tell lies on God that you believe in, and some of you preach.

The Sins you do day in and day out.

<u>Sins like:</u>
Adultery
Murder
Theft
Burglary which is theft as well
Incest
And more.

Therefore, no one is free to live because the Constitutions of Men protect not the citizens but, protect the different levels of government and their friends; Corporate Demons, and Religious Demons that plague the Earth thus, many get away with murder.

*As Black people, we have to; must wake up and know that we are truly not protected by the Laws and different Laws of Men; the White Race and the different races.*

*If we as Black People do not truly unite, we will not be saved.*

Now to interrupt this book and I have not yet fully and truly begun to edit it.

It's August 25, 2021, and I have to sound the more than Critical Alarm to what I am seeing via my dream world.

*Yes, Technology is the <u>DEATH OF HUMANS</u>.*

Humans are truly not seeing what is going on around them.

*If you as a human think you are safe and protected; you are truly not protected to what I see with Robotics.*

Humans are going to be eradicated shortly more, and more.

<u>Covid-19 is just the first stage – the Mark of the Beast.</u>

<u>Global Starvation is the other.</u>

<u>*Robotic Elimination is the other.*</u> *Meaning, humans being eliminated by robots.*

*So, all you see they are doing Robotics Wise via man's so-called technology is their final elimination and or, eradication of humans.*

<u>*I cannot tell you where this lab is because I truly don't know.*</u>

I've seen a lot, told you a lot of what I see via my dreams and waking state visions, but this place truly stumps me.

Yes, God is my rescue to what I see.

*Your Political Leaders cannot help you because, none of your Political Leaders run Earth; the Globe. They; your Political Leaders have to; must take their orders from the higher up. I do not care who you call these people, and don't even think your billionaires because; your billionaires are just puppets; brainwashed trolls and minions who lack knowledge and education for those who run and own them. Therefore, I see beyond what you see.*

I will not get into Cloning, nor will I get into Mind Control because this great power he seeks is greater than man. Thus, the Beast of Man, and the Realm Beyond God that humans know not about. And I am going to leave it there because what I know, you truly do not know.

<u>*AMEN*</u> *by the Reggae Artist Luciano.*

*Truly listen to the lyrics of this song. Right and True Knowledge is one of the Keys to Life.*

Michelle
August 2021

Oh God I know
I know

These are the days when I feel helpless with the knowledge that is open to me. Thus, I will leave my Technology; Robotics Dream alone.

Humans are doomed because the Technology of Man was not meant to preserve life, but to *"KILL ALL LIFE HERE ON EARTH."*

Yes, some will say Rebirth, but absolutely nothing can be reborn again once it's been born.

This too I am going to leave alone because something is truly not right with my analogy of Rebirth.

So, what I truly do not know, let me leave it alone because; *"A GREAT DEATH – PURGE – MASSACRE"* is coming, and going to be on Earth.

Thus, I do not know what **"not for I"** truly mean. Those words I saw this morning before me written in black; bold black on white paper with lowercase writing. This was not a dream but a waking state vision.

Lovey, truly help me because I truly need help. I see Lovey but, I am helpless to do here on Earth therefore; I need your help here on Earth Lovey truthfully.


Michelle
August 25, 2021

It's August 27, 2021 Lovey and to the way I feel, I have no hope this morning to the dream I had.

Lovey, these people that design, create, and manufacture the different weapons, diseases, viruses, and more. *"DO THEY NOT THINK OF THEIR SOUL?"*

*"DO THEY NOT THINK OF THEIR HELL IN HELL?"*

No Lovey, *"THE SICKEST RACE ON THE FACE OF THIS PLANET IN MY VIEW IS THE WHITE RACE NO MATTER THE COLOUR OF SKIN, HAIR TYPE, EYE COLOUR, GENDER, RELIGIOUS DENOMINATION, RELIGIOUS AFFILIATION, AND MORE."*

*"HOW DO THESE MONSTERS LIVE WITH THEMSELVES?"*

No Lovey, I am going to go as far as this, and Mother Earth truly forgive me because I am hurt, truly hurt this morning.

Lovey, forgive me also.

But Mother Earth, *"HOW DO YOU LIVE WITH YOURSELF?"*

*"HOW DO YOU LOOK AT YOURSELF DAY IN AND DAY OUT KNOWING YOU HAVE AND*

<u>HAS GIVEN THE WICKED AND EVIL A HOME HERE ON EARTH?"</u>

<u>"HOW DO YOU LOOK AT LIFE MOTHER EARTH?"</u>

<u>"HOW DO YOU EVEN FORGIVE YOU KNOWING THAT YOU AIDE AND ABED DEATH IN YOU?"</u>

Earth has become vile, evil, wicked worse than Sodom and Gomorrah of man's so-called Holy Bible due to humans, and you continue to let this happen.

Humans use you, defile you, curse you, take all life from you, and more.

<u>"HOW CAN GOD; LOVEY AND I TRUST YOU TO DO ALL THAT IS RIGHT IN YOU FOR THE BETTER GOOD OF LIFE?"</u>

I am sorry Mother Earth, but I had to; have to question your truth and loyalty for life; good and true life.

Yes, this had to do with the dream I had this morning and or, last night.

<u>2000 Black Kids; Children died, and my Dream World would not let me go of this dream.</u>

I do not know if the 2000 deaths had to do with the Children taking the Covid-19 Vaccine, but 2000 Kids; Black Kids died Mother Earth. Yes, it hurts because Black People are not seeing what is going on.

*I am helpless to help.*
*I have no land.*
*No water.*
*No food.*
*No nothing and or, anything.*

I don't even have a passport.

I am stuck here in Babylon without any escape, and this too truly hurt me.

I can't anymore with you and God because neither of you see my urgent need.

Neither of you; you Mother Earth and Lovey is securing a true place for me and the saved.

I am losing hope Lovey.
I am losing hope Mother Earth.

## 2000 Black Children.

Yes, 2000 is reminiscent of Jesus for some. But 2000 Black Children dead just like that!!!!

No Lovey and Mother Earth.

## "HOW DO WHITE PEOPLE LIVE WITH THEMSELVES KNOWING THEY ARE MURDERERS?"

## "HOW DO THEY LIVE WITH THEMSELVES KNOWING THEY LIVE TO KILL AND ARE KILLING?"

No Lovey, it has to be over. I cannot take it anymore.

## 2000 Black Children dropping out – dying just like that Lovey!!!!!!

*Lovey, I do not know where if it's in the United States of Death; America, the Caribbean, South America, or Africa these deaths are going to occur but Lovey, 2000 Black Children dead just like that!!!!*

No, I have to question the integrity of Mother Earth, and all Black People here on Earth.

*I can't just blame Mother Earth, I have to* **BLAME BLACK PEOPLE AND OUR TRUTH AND LOYALTY TO ONE ANOTHER BECAUSE, I AM TRULY HURT TO THE POINT OF WANTING TO CRY.**

So no, I truly do not know.

*I do not know if some* <u>SICK PSYCHOPATH</u> *is going to go on a rampage and start killing Black kids.*

No Lovey, Mentally Sick are People especially those in the White Race thus, I have no compassion for murderers; those who willingly and knowingly take life at will to please their perverse and demented self, and leaders.

---

Lovey, Mother Earth, Black People, *2000 Black Children gaane jus suh!!!*

Dear God, have mercy on my soul.

*Thus, humans need to look into the Vaccines of Death Globally especially the Moderna Vaccine.*

Michelle

It is sad for me Lovey and Mother Earth because Blacks still do not get it. And yes, I am learning.

2000 Black Children dying represents Death. *THE DEATH OF BLACK PEOPLE.*

*WE AS BLACK PEOPLE REPRESENT JESUS OF THEIR BIBLE.*

Yes, 2000 years when Blacks must die; be crucified.

Black People have not put this together; hence, the religious beliefs of Blacks globally.

*Religion was used as a WEAPON TO KILL US, AND RELIGION DID KILL BLACKS PHYSICALLY AND SPIRITUALLY.*

*RIVERS OF BABYLON by the Reggae Artist Luciano.*

*If we as Black People do not unify truthfully and help ourselves, we will be slaughtered again.*

*2000 years is up.* The slaughtering must begin shortly on a massive scale.

If you as Black People refuse to listen this time around, you will be doomed. You as Black People will never get out of Slavery, and you will forever weep and sing; *"THE RIVERS OF BABYLON."*

*You as Black People:*

*"REFUSE TO LISTEN."*

*"YOU REFUSE TO FIND YOUR TRUTH."*

*"YOU REFUSE TO FIND YOUR TRUE BLACK GOD."*

*"YOU REFUSE TO LET GO OF THE WHITE WAY."*

*"DEATH AND LIFE IS NOT ONE."* Therefore, Black People find your Black God and way in life.

Michelle
August 27, 2021

Now tell me Lovey and Mother Earth.

What do we do because Black People aren't getting it?

Yes, I am at a loss because I do see.

I am learning, but how do I get Black People to receive the truth and live?

*Blacks have been colonized.*
*Brainwashed*
*Given lies*
*Given religious lies*

We of our self have and has tainted our life story, our past, our present, our future, and our tomorrow.

So yes, Black People have become weapons because we know not the truth of us, the truth of life, the truth of self, the truth of Earth, the Sky, Moon, Universe, and more we know not the truth.

Michelle
August 27, 2021

Lovey we need to Move Up
We need to move forward
We need to be safe.

We need to truly move on.

With what I am seeing Dream Wise Lovey, we have to move to a safe place with our good and true people only.

We cannot save the wicked and evil of Earth.

We have to; must save our good and true own only.

As we move forward Lovey; the pleasure and beauty of planting with you, I truly need to plant some more.

With all that is happening Lovey, why aren't Black People taking heed?

Why aren't Black People globally waking up?

Why aren't Black People globally truly doing for self?

Why are Black People globally still governed by White Lies?

Why are we as Black People holding on to Death's Way?

Oh wow. The Eradication Order; Kill Switch is here but, Black People are truly too caught up in the Covid-19 distraction that none know they are going to be killed. Have to be killed.

*Michelle*
*August 2021*

Lovey, my Selenite Crystal broke.
What am I going to do now?

Lovey, are you going to leave me naked now?

Are you going to tell me what to do now?

Right now, all I know is; I truly want to continue to plant good and true with you.

It is beautiful planting with you.

The pleasure I get from planting is truly great. So, can we continue to plant good and true with each other?

Lovey, I need the right soil now.

I truly need the right soil.

No Lovey. When I look around, I see no true growth Vegetable and Plant Wise. Everything is dying including that which I planted good and true with you Lovey.

Why?

Michelle
August 14, 2021

There is so much that I want to say Lovey.

Right now, apart from planting good and true with you. How about travel for Black People because if you want to travel, you have to accept the *MARK OF THE BEAST* Lovey. And I refuse this.

*I refuse to take their Mark – Vaccination.*

Now Lovey tell me, why do you and Mother Earth continue to let the wicked and evil; Evil Politicians – all Politicians, Corporate Greed, and Pharmaceutical Greed take life from you, the good and true, and truly trying to be good?

How do we escape the Law and Laws of these demons who run the globe?

Lovey, I truly feel forsaken because I cannot travel.

Lovey, why is my Human and Life Rights being taken from me?

Lovey what about us?

I don't want their Mark Lovey, but how do we travel as I truly do not have access to space, speed, time – all the avenues to get from Point A to Point B without the Apparatuses of Man; Men?

How do I get to South Africa if I have not the technology to do so?

How do I travel with you Lovey if I have no means to travel?

Black Lands are no different from White Lands. Black People follow the Law and Laws of the White Race; Death.

Black Lands are Corporate Owned because many – you know what Lovey – ALL BLACK POLITICIANS KISS THE ASS OF WHITE PEOPLE thus, Black Lands are not governed by BLACK LAWS, they are governed by White Laws, and Corporate Laws.

No Lovey let's be real. WHAT BLACK LAWS DO BLACK LANDS GOVERN UNDER OR BY?

WHAT BLACK LAWS DO BLACK PEOPLE LIVE UNDER OR BY?

WHAT FREEDOM DO BLACK LANDS HAVE?

Lovey, I am truly tired of:
- White Rule
- White Lies
- White Laws
- White Power
- All that is White
- Evil
- And deceitful.

Lovey, why can't we as Black People be Black?

Why can't we as Black People live by our own Black Laws?

---

- *Govern by our own Black Laws?*
- *Have our own Black God back; you Lovey*
- *Live Black*
- *Be Black*
- *Be true and truly Black*
- *Live Black Right*
- *Live Black Honest and True*
- *And more Good and True Things.*

Aye Lovey, truly thank you for making me a true and good Black Person; Woman.


Michelle
August 2021

*Lovey, with all that is going on with Covid-19 and their Vaccines of Death. Why can't Black Lands come together truthfully and break away from White Society, the White Way of doing things?*

Why are Blacks Falla Batties Lovey?

*Why can't we as Blacks have our own Black Passport independent of other Passports that we as Blacks; Black People only can use to travel to the different Black Lands in Africa, South America, Central America, the Caribbean, and more?*

*No Lovey, I was thinking about this this morning. The Passport can either be Yellow and Green or just Yellow or Green with trees, and a water fall between the trees to signify our TRUE BOND AND LIFE WITH YOU LOVEY, AND WITH US AS A RACE AND PEOPLE.*

Our Black Passport no other race can use or get.

This Passport is for True Black People only. Not even Fake Blacks can use this new Passport Lovey come on now.

This Passport should also signify our new and true beginning with you Lovey come on now.

## <u>Lovey, why can't Blacks live independent and not dependent?</u>

*Why can't Blacks open their eyes and stop being fooled?*

*Lovey, I am at a crossroad. Just all out disgusted to see the different nations being forced to take a vaccine that many do not want. And what gets to me is that,* <u>we as Blacks refuse to unify peacefully and true and come together and have our on true Black Economy.</u>

Michelle
August 2021

So yes Lovey, I feel hopeless.
Feel abandoned.
Feel victimized.

Because the White Race of Bullies, Liars, and Thieves have and has condemned life here on Earth to Death.

No Lovey. Life is worth living. It's evil; wicked and evil people that are making people die for Death.

Come on Lovey. What Life Rights are there on Earth for us as Black People?

*What Lovey and or, God Rights do we as Black People here on Earth have?*

*What Lovey and or, God Rights do you Lovey have here on Earth?*

*Now tell me Lovey,* **with all that is happening here on Earth; can you and I bypass Death?**

Did Death's Children and People not make sure Earth is uninhabitable for you Lovey, Me, the good and true, and the truly trying to be good?

Yes, my hope is fading because; I have no way to turn apart from turning to you Lovey. I cannot live with or amongst the Domain of the Dead Lovey come on now.

*Where is our place here on Earth Lovey that is void of:*
*White Laws*
*White Lies*
*White Entitlement*
*The destruction of the Waterways*

*The destruction of all life here on Earth*
*Death*
*And more wicked and evil things.*


Michelle
August 2021

It's August 15th Lovey, and I am at a crossroad. I do not know if I should start a new book with just dreams, or put these dreams in this book.

Last night was a night of my Muscle Spasms acting up. They were not bad, but I had them anyway.

Lovey, how do I shut down the chatter – negative chatter in my brain?

I am trying to connect with my inner me, and my brain and or, external forces that can manipulate my brain negatively are refusing to let me connect to myself – my higher self.

Lovey, why do things have to be so hard for me?

Why can't my life be easy now?

Why are things so slow for me gaining wise, finding the right mate, and more?

Right now, I am craving happiness. I need to meet the right someone for us, and it is truly hard for me; why?

You know what let me let that go and get into my dreams because; *Death was all around me.*

*Death was telling me someone is going to die in my family.*

I do not know if it's my cousin in America or my uncle in Jamaica on my mother's side, but someone is going to die. *Death did confirm this with me.*

I am so not going to worry. 2021 is the Year of Death and Destruction and it is only going to get worse.

So not going to worry about humans because we; humans are the cause of all this.

*Humans do not think of the future.*

*Humans do not think of Earth or the Future of Earth.*

*Humans do not think of future generations.*

*Humans do not maintain or sustain Earth.*

*In all humans do, they do all to destroy Earth.*

*In all humans do, humans do not think of their Sins.*

*Do not think nor do they know that their Sins affect Life here on Earth including Earth herself.*

*Do not think or know that our Sins contribute to the decay; Death of Earth thus, the destruction globally that is happening here on Earth. So, no, I will not worry about humans because humans are Primitive, Destructive by Nature in my view Lovey. Thus, Death was around me, and me seeing this Black Man; slender in Gray lying face up. He had died.*

So, yes, the Death Toll of Black Males and Females is going to rise.

## Did I dream about Drake the Canadian Rapper this morning August 15, 2021?

Yes

I was with my dad and a baby in the dream.

We were walking in the Keele Hwy 7 region going West.

Walking with my dad and the baby, we came to this area where Drake and this other Black Guy, Young Black Guy was walking.

They were conversing together as they walked, and my dad went to lay in the grass and or, on the ground. It was as if he was tired. As for the baby, I truly do not know what happened to the child. The baby was not with us anymore.

The Young Black Guy with Drake had a book in his hand. Think Bible like book.

Oh Lord. Judgement because; Black People are going to be judged shortly.

Allelujah. Judgement

*Dear God. If we as Black People do not begin; start unifying, we will not; never escape that which is to come because, Death is going to start judging literally.*

## Onwards I go

I could not read the words in his book *though the book was open.*

The book was not for me to read people.

---

I know what this book is in real life.

You know what let me finish the dream and then talk if not talk in-between because; many – *ALL IN THE MUSIC INDUSTRY HAVE AND HAS BEEN DECEIVED.* In the dream, I told Drake; *"HE SOLD HIS SOUL."* *He did not disagree; he said, he was "safe – saved,"*

*I told him he was not safe – saved. Once he sold his soul, Satan owns him, his family. He was shocked; did not believe me.*

*I told him read what is said in Revelations about Jews, and re-iterated Syn, and Synagogue.*

*Shensea's name also came up. He brought up her NAME OF SELLING HER SOUL AS WELL.*

I so can't remember if the Young Black Guy with Drake scrolled and or, went to Revelations in his book.

No, he didn't *BECAUSE; BLACK DEATH WALKS WITH DRAKE AND IS RECORDING EVERYTHING HE DOES LITERALLY.*

*In the dream, did I want to say: Jay-Z and Beyonce sold their souls as well?*

Yes, but did not get the chance to.

*Michelle*

Now let me clarify things to you in the Entertainment Industry as well as, you in Scientology from other books because obviously none of you got the Memo or Message.

*"YOU ARE ALL BEING LIED TO."*

*Now let me double quote it.*

*""YOU ARE ALL BEING LIED TO.""*

*I will and can triple quote it.*

*"""YOU ARE ALL BEING LIED TO."""*

IF YOU HAVE SOLD YOUR SOUL. YES, SIGNED ON THE DOTTED LINE OF DEATH – YOUR CONTRACT, PERFORMED YOUR RITUAL; DEATH OWNS YOU.

**YOUR FAMILY, YOUR MONEY, HOUSES, CARS; EVERYTHING IS OWNED BY DEATH.**

**YOU CANNOT BE SAVED AND WILL NEVER BE SAVED.**

# YOUR HOME AFTER YOUR SPIRIT SHED THE FLESH IS HELL. *There are no ands, ifs, or buts about this.*

It matters not the sacrifice; you belong to Death.

A Child of Life cannot save you.

As for Shensea, she is of Babylonian Descent therefore, I do not know how rituals work for them; Indians and Mixed-Raced Indians because; they are not apart of Life.

But because her lineage is Jamaican; she was born under the Banner of Life despite Jamaica being owned by Female Death, I truly do not know.

I do not know if the ritual she did, and the sacrifice she made sticks. She is not saved anyway due to her Babylonian Heritage and Lineage.

Now, the Jews you see claiming to be Jews are truly not Jews. THEY ARE OF THE SYNAGOGUE OF SATAN thus, Revelations of Death; your so-called Holy Bible.

You were told these Jews are Satan's Children but, many of you overlooked this main fact.

*<u>These Jews are Satan's Children that emulate the True White Jews that was then but truly not now except for 1 that I know of but he's Nasty as F. Need to truly clean self up if he and his family want or need to be saved.</u>*

The True Jews are Young Black Females with nappy, happy, as pappy kinky hair like mine.

Their hair is cut low with the exception of 1 mixed; bi-racial child of Black and White Mixture.

How it was originally set up. White Jews were to protect Black Jews – the Children of Life. And yes, this is why you have White People on the Mountain of Life; God. Not many.

*I only saw 1 sickly White Male on the Mountain <u>as NO WHITES ARE AT THE TOP OF THE MOUNTAIN WITH GOD.</u> They are in the middle thus, Africa. Africa being the Center of Life or the Universe if you want to put it that way and or, the Birthplace of Death.*

*This is why Africa is significant to Whites when it's all said and done. Death have to go back to Death; find their home in that way.*

Now, I am off track.

Listen, True Jews – True Black Jews that were/are born under the Black Banner of Life is not; <u>"TRULY NOT GOVERNED BY THE LAW AND LAWS OF DEATH. THEY ARE GOVERNED BY THE LAW AND LAWS OF LIFE."</u> This is why Drake said he was safe –

saved. But and or, however; "<u>Drake is truly not saved.</u>"

# "WHITE JEWS CANNOT SAVE ANYONE."

<u>They hath no authority to save anyone under the Law and Laws of Life.</u>

God did not choose White Jews to save anyone. <u>God chose and have to choose or chose "A BLACK FEMALE." One who is of Life to save the Children and People of Life here on Earth.</u>

God cannot save Death's Children and People, nor can God save those who have sold their Soul to Death; Satan.

Nor can God save so-called White Jews, or all those who belong to the different dominations of Religion. You're all of Death. Therefore, Drake; Death; Black Male Death walks with you and records all that you do. Therefore, your name is in the Book of Death and not in the Book of Life.

And yes, I am seeing your Death because; I do see the hell, <u>and death of some long before they die.</u>

<u>Here on Earth, I do have access to Hell and Death thus, my sight; what I can see, and do see.</u>

Michelle
August 15, 2021

Let me interrupt my writings now.

White Jews did forfeit their Life with God. Hence their Six-Pointed Star. Them joining forces with Death.

## <u>Life goes up not down therefore:</u>

# IT IS STRICTLY FORBIDDEN TO JOIN THE UPRIGHT TRIANGLE OF LIFE WITH THE DOWNWARD TRIANGLE OF DEATH.

<u>*Triangles are significant to Life, and yes, Death.*</u>

Now, those monstrosities that you see on the Internet under Images in Google is truly not what Satan looks like.

*Satan, if you put all the most handsomest Males on Earth and put them together, they could not compare to the beauty – handsomeness of Satan. Satan is a hottie, hot, hot, hottie. That gorgeous.*

He's also White with Black Hair.

In some of my earlier books I did describe Satan. **NOR**

# DOES SATAN HAVE 666 ON HIS FOREHEAD.

## <u>666 IS ON SATAN'S SIDE.</u>

I can't remember if it's on his right side but one of my much earlier books tell you which side.

## <u>SATAN DID PROCREATE WITH A BLACK FEMALE.</u> *Hence Satan has 3 bi-racial daughters. They are triplets that walk-in unison, and each daughter; child has a 6 in their forehead; hence, the 666. And I did explain this and more in my much earlier books.*

*Even in Hell in his burning state Satan is still handsome.*

So, it is truly wise not to interlock or lock the upright and downward triangle.

In regard to the 666. Each 6 represent 6000 years. Each of Satan's daughters time here on Earth to deceive.

3 Daughters; Triplets = 18 which is 6+6+6.

Satan is 1 = 6

Satan's mate do not come into play. She was just the bearer of his/Satan's Children. No time was allotted to her as far as I know.

Satan 6

Satan's Daughters 666

## <u>Now add</u>

You should get 24.

24000 Years Satan had. Which is 24000 Earth Years, and 1 day in Spiritual Time.

And no. Satan cannot get more time nor can Satan claim:

666 + 666 which is 1332

And no, I am not going to relate this 1332 to 1313 which is a date, or the dates in the Book of Daniel in your so-called Holy Bible.

As 19 is Symbolic to for some Muslims, I will leave well enough alone.

*So, 24000 years or 24 refers to Army Time – the TIME OF DEATH. So, 24 is a reminder for Death's People thus, the TIME TO DIE; KILL. And I am going to stop here because I did cover this in other books.*

*Onwards I go with this book.*

Michelle
August 16, 2021

Lovey, as Black People our belief systems have to; must change.

As Black People, if we do not know the truth; how are we going to live tomorrow?

How are we going to find our way?

As Black People, if we know not our true roots; how are we going to find you Lovey?

As Black People, we have to; must find our way.

*We have to; must unify true.*

We cannot say we are Black and not know the truth, and full truth of who we are as individuals, and a Race and People.

No Lovey. As Blacks and or, Black People; we cannot keep integrating and fighting for, and with Systems that are truly not our own.

We can't keep fighting with self and each other either.

It's time we as Black People recognize and realize the different Systems of Men were never ever meant for us.

Thus, it's time to stop talking and live right.

*STOP TALKING - Fiona*

*Michelle Jean*
*August 15, 2021*

Black People, we have to come together and help ourself including save self.

We can no longer sacrifice ourselves for the benefit of the different races.

We can no longer sacrifice ourselves for the benefit of the different religions, and religious gods out there.

We have to start truly doing for self.

We have to start living good and true with each other.

We have to start sustaining and maintaining self and each other.


Michelle
August 15, 2021

Allelujah help me
Hold on to me
Bless me
Bless my hand
Truly help me to heal me
Truly help me to heal others

Allelujah, God and Lovey; truly help me to build us good and true.

Truly see with me and truly help me.

Truly give me the strength and power to make true changes that are positive in the lives of all who come in contact with me, read these words, and more.

Allelujah, Lovey and God, be true and good to me all the time.


Michelle
August 15, 2021

Lovey, what about my Life Rights and Human Rights?

Are you telling me, you are going to willingly hand me over to Death just like that?

Are you as God – Good God and Allelujah telling me, you are just going to hand our people over to Death, and the Children and People of Death just like that?

You won Lovey. You have your book, and you have your plant. So, let's stand in victory and gather our people to a safe place where they do not have to live with the different Criminals of Society.

No Lovey. As Black People, your true and good own; we cannot have different sets of Laws for the different races because, we are now one people living under your true and good banner.

Our Societies and Living Space cannot be like man; men.

We have to have clean living spaces Lovey come on now.

But with you winning Lovey, my mind is still fearful.

Why is it so hard to shut down the Devil right away?

Why am I lacking hope today?

Why do I feel as if Knowledge Wise I have failed?

Why do I feel lost because the onset of Covid-19 and their Vaccines of Death is out there?

No Lovey. Where is my Human Rights?

<u>*I should not be forced to take a vaccine nor is it right or just for any leader to force Death on their people. So now Lovey, how fair are you?*</u>

I know you are fair. I am just truly scared because I do not want to die. I truly need you.

*Lovey, I truly do not want or need their* <u>**MARK OF THE BEAST.**</u> *Thus, their* <u>**MARK OF DEATH – COVID-19, AND THEIR COVID-19 VACCINES.**</u>


Michelle
August 16, 2021

I should not fear Lovey, but I do fear for my life.

Yes, I want and need better but does better want and need me?

*I fear not for the lives of Blacks because; you've shown me time and time again, Blacks will not receive me. Thus, the Lies of the Many – different races – Devils suit them just fine.*

Yes, its sad that you've been trying to save us, but it's us as a Race and People that continually abandon life yet say, they are oppressed and want to be saved.

We as Blacks refuse to come out of oppression. We continually sit and stay in the shit; lies we are given.

*We've become complacent and lazy life wise.*
*We've become complacent and Lovey; God Wise.*

*We keep sitting on our ass and expect Lovey; God to do all for us.*

Right now Lovey, I know I am the only one with you here on Earth in my view.

I am the only one in your world here on Earth in my view. And Lovey, if I am wrong, please let me know, and forgive me as there are no other Blacks with me. Sad yes, but this is my reality.

Blacks want Life but are truly not willing to let go of the life they have right now.

*Blacks have been colonized Lovey.*
*Blacks do sell out their own Blacks.*
*Blacks do praise and worship Death.*

Blacks did become captured souls; the slaves to Death, and the Children and People of Death.


Michelle
August 2021

*So, as I talk to you my way Lovey in prayer and in goodness and truth.*

*Where do we belong on this day Lovey?*
*Where do we belong?*

*I am truly scared.*

*I don't know if you feel my pain – scaredness but I am truly scared.*

*Truly Lovey do not let my enemies and your enemies devour me.*

*Right now, I wish I had the key to another world. Yes, that Key to open the portal to another world where I can escape the ills of this world, and the further ills to come.*

*Lovey, why does Earth have to be overrun by wicked and evil beings?*

*Why are certain thing not right away with you Lovey?*

*Why do I have to live in fear because of them; the wicked and evil?*

*My heart and truth for you is pure yet, I feel your heart and truth for me is truly not pure on this day. Yes, this is due to my fears.*

*Yes, you are God but today, <u>you being God is not enough for me.</u> Please do not ask me why because I truly do not know.*

*You truly haven't failed me, nor do I doubt you. I am just in a different place right now. Yes, that place where I truly want and need all evil to be shut down here on Earth where I can live in truth and true peace with you Lovey.*

*Michelle*
*August 17, 2021*

Aye Lovey, I have the opportunity to go on the Nikki Clarke Show in September, and I am hoping you are there with me.

Hoping you truly bless me.
Keep me safe.

Allow me to speak our truth with true eloquence, true passion, true love, true everything.

Lovey, I truly need you to be my voice, my hope, my reasoning; all that is true within me, you, around me, around you, and more good and true things.

Lovey, truly *BLESS THIS DAY, SEPTEMBER 22, 2021,* and let all good things happen for me, you, and her; Nikki Clarke.

*Lovey, this is a true start for us; so truly have compassion for Nikki Clarke, and truly bless her life rewardingly. I truly thank her and hope you be with her Lovey.*

Lovey and God, mark September 22, 2021, on our calendar of goodness and truth, and let nothing negative happen for us on this day.

Lovey, I pray that you sit with me.
Let everything be positive.
Blessed
Good
True
Ever growing up good and true.

Lovey, I truly need you with me.

Lovey, let the audience grow on this day for her.

Lovey, this is my one shot, and I pray that you bless Nikki, her show, the people that are around her, the people who watch her show, and more on this day September 22, 2021, with pure goodness and positivity; pure growth, and more good and true things.

Lovey and God, favour us on this day, and truly be our good and true reward and source.

Michelle
August 2021

With that said Lovey.
Truly be my feet
Right and left hand
My good and true all.

Lovey, truly be the decision maker in all of this because I am making you my good and true Agent, and Publicist in all of this.

Yes Lovey, I need you to be my true more.

Lovey, we planted together therefore, I know the true goodness of you.

Now tell me. Why can't this goodness and truth engulf my life and surround me and you daily without end?

Lovey, am I the only one here on Earth that can feel your goodness and truth?

Please let me know.


Michelle
August 17, 2021

You know what is so sad about humans Lovey. *Many kill for Control and Territorial Control.*

Tell me Lovey. What does Control profit apart from Death?

What peace can anyone find in Death Lovey?

Why die here on Earth to die a brutal death in Hell?

Why imprison yourself in Hell here on Earth?

Do humans not know they are the ones to create their own Prison – Hell?

As humans, why can't we think correctly?

Earth have to cleanse Earth therefore, all the evils of man – humans is further solidifying their place in Hell.


Michelle
August 17, 2021

It's August 17, 2021 and truly thank you Lovey.
Truly thank you for you.

Truly thank you for providing for me.

Today, wow. Thank you for providing my needs.

Aye Lovey, truly thank you because you are my true way in life.

*True comfort*
*True provider*
*True all*

Lovey, truly continue to let our seeds grow.

Lovey, let the June Plum I plant catch, be sweet, be ever healing, good for us and our body, truly loving and fruitful, and more good and true things.

Lovey, as I think of all these books that I have written, and continue to write with your truth, and true help; truly let these books be true and good food for all who read them.

Lovey, Knowledge is key to and for the both of us therefore, truly let everyone find Knowledge, Truth, True Healing, and True Blessings from them; these books.

Lovey, truly be my good and true love, guide, Mountain of Goodness and Truth, Good and True Life that I come to all the time for advice, truth, true love, true life, and more.

*Michelle*

God is good all the time.

I haven't been writing as of late. Spending a lot of time playing games. I truly don't know Lovey because I am tired of living here on Earth on this day.

No Lovey, what is wrong with Black People?

Lovey, why can't every Black Person come together and develop Black Lands?

*No Lovey,* WHY CAN'T EVERY BLACK PERSON SAY F IT AND JUST COME TOGETHER COLLECTIVELY AND JUST SEEK ASYLUM IN AFRICA, AND OTHER BLACK LANDS, AND LEAVE RACIST WHITE AMERICANS TO THEIR OWN DOOM?

*No Lovey,* IT'S TIME WHITE PEOPLE FIGHT AMONGST EACH OTHER WHERE WE AS BLACK PEOPLE ARE SAFE AND AWAY FROM THEM; WHITES.

*So Lovey,* CAN WE RESURRECT THE BLACK AND OR, BACK TO AFRICA MOVEMENT AND LET ALL BLACK PEOPLE FIND A PLACE IN AFRICA, OR OTHER BLACK LANDS, AND BAN ALL WHITE PEOPLE FROM ENTERING OUR LAND AND LANDS MORE THAN FOREVER EVER WITHOUT END?

*No Lovey, I am fed up of White Entitlement.*

*Fed up of the way Earth is being run by White People.*
*Tired of White Bullshit that they force on People globally.*

*Fed up of living around them; White People that lie and deceive.*

Lovey, what is wrong with Black People?

*Why can't I enact true change for* <u>GOOD AND TRUE</u>
<u>BLACKS HERE ON EARTH LOVEY?</u>

*Lovey, look at the way Black Americans are treated yet, they sit in the shit they are in. It's time we as Black People leave out of lands that oppress us, kill us, cause us to lose our self worth, integrity, soul, and more.*

*No Lovey, I am depending on you, and you are truly failing me in this where; I want and need to be in our environment of truth.*

*I've seen a Earth without White People Lovey. So, why is it taking so long to bypass this race and let their evils consume them where;* <u>TRUE BLACK PEOPLE ARE LIVING</u>
<u>WITH YOU IN OUR LAND VOID OF ALL ILLS;</u>
<u>SINS, AND WICKEDNESS INCLUDING,</u>
<u>WICKED AND EVIL PEOPLE?</u>

Lovey, why is things so hard?

I do not comprehend why people cannot see the evils around them.

No Lovey there is so much to talk to you about.

I am seeing faces before me again. I am not going to worry about these faces because I know this is Death's way of showing who they are going to take from Earth.

I cannot worry about Death in this way.

*Lovey, I don't want to think. But life is truly beautiful with you. And yes,* I want to start a WORLD PETITION TO CHARGE THE DIFFERENT GOVERNMENTS, AND PHARMACEUTICAL COMPANIES FOR GENOCIDE.

*Lovey,* THE DIFFERENT GOVERNMENTS OF THE WORLD ARE NO DIFFERENT FROM TERRORISTS.

*They in the Western Hemisphere talk about terrorists and the Governments of the West including Pharmaceutical Greed; Demons and Corporate Demons and greed, are nothing more than Terrorists.*

*Humans have no human rights here on Earth because you are being forced to take a Vaccine that hurt you, and is not even effective in curing the same virus they created in labs.*

*No Lovey,* IT IS EVIL THAT ARE KILLING PEOPLE HERE ON EARTH YET, WESTERN LANDS ARE NOT PAYING THE PRICE FOR THEIR ILLS IN MY VIEW.

*No, the little fires, water, volcanoes, and more happening globally is truly not enough in my view.*

*Thus, I do not know why it is taking so long to separate all evil from all who are good?*

*Lovey, good cannot reside under the Law and Laws of Evil come on now.*

*Lovey, good cannot be under the same roof as the wicked and evil.*

*So Lovey,* <u>*I am coming to you because you are the*</u> <u>*HIGHEST COURT OF JUSTICE I CAN GO TO.*</u>

<u>*YOU HAVE YOUR BOOK AND BOOKS.*</u>
<u>*YOU HAVE YOUR SEED PLANTED.*</u>

<u>*Let it be done now for all who are wicked and evil.*</u>

We have to start the exodus.

We have to protect and secure the good and true of life here on Earth now Lovey come on now.

Satan's Children and People did fulfill their bible. It's time we Lovey secure our people from the evils to come more.

It's time for the Good in Life and of Life to secure our life.

*It's time for Good to fulfill our book and books by living right, good and true, doing right good and true, separating and segregating right good and true from all of Death's Wicked and Evil Own; People, Spirits, Negative Energy, Negative Forces, and more.*

<u>*LOVEY, YOU CANNOT SEE MY TRUE AND*</u> <u>*PASSIONATE NEED FOR CHANGE LOVEY*</u> <u>*AND IGNORE ME.*</u>

*I am so passionate for change when it comes to Covid-19 that I want and need to start a online petition but, I need your Green Light and Permission Lovey. I need you, the Moon, Mother Earth, the Universe, all around me, including Death to stand with me on this Lovey. I cannot do it without you all.*

*No one should be forced to take Vaccines for diseases created by humans Lovey come on now.*

*No Lovey, why are humans creating viruses, chemicals, and diseases that kill?*

*No Lovey, when I do wrong, I am punished right away yet, evil people rule the Earth and get away with their evil deeds.*

*Lovey, I am truly passionate about life, but don't force things on people.*

Come on Lovey, I need my life. Why should I give up my life to Death because of Wicked and Evil People?

*No Lovey, why is it that Mother Earth isn't crumbling the buildings of these Mega Corporations of Greed and letting the Shareholders, and Owners suffer financially?*

I know Lovey I sound evil but in truth, I need you, and it truly hurts to see people wanting to take you from me life wise, and more.

*I can't travel without their vaccine.*

*Some can't work without their vaccine.*
*Some can't go to school without their vaccine.*
*How fair and just is this Lovey?*

*No Mother Earth, how fair and just is this all around?*

*No man I am tired of White Entitlement.*
*I am tired of the way in which Earth is being run.*

*I am tired of living under colonial rule.*
*Tired of living under lies and injustice.*
*Tired of not being free.*

No Lovey, why are you allowing Devils to take my rights and freedom from me?

Why are you allowing Devils to let me lose you?

Why are you allowing Devils to continue to control and run Earth?

Where is my life rights here on Earth?

So yes, I need to have a petition.

I need your good and true backing.
I need you to truly support me.

I need you to sign my petition. I can't lose you come on now.

Do you not feel how I feel?
Are you not concerned for my life?

Mother Earth, I am reaching out to you also. *Are you not concerned for my life?*

Are you not a part of True Life here on Earth?

Why is evil; the evils of humans ruining you?
Why do you allow it to happen?

I am scared. I don't know what else to do.

I truly can't lose life here on Earth or in the Spiritual Realm.

There is so much that I want and need to do. I am just discovering the pleasure and beauty of planting with Lovey, and I truly do not want or need this pleasure and beauty to stop. But how do I help you and Lovey if the Devil is let loose in you Mother Earth?

How do we shut the Devil and different Devils down here on Earth and or, in you Mother Earth?

*No Lovey and Mother Earth, there are people out there who know the truth but are scared to talk. I talk in these books but now I truly need to take this passion further by starting a petition online against Covid-19, and the Vaccine. Lovey, the Spiritual Realm reminded me of the* DEATH THAT IS ASSOCIATED WITH COVID-19 AND THE VACCINE(S) ASSOCIATED WITH THIS TREATH.

LOVE FROM A DISTANCE - Beres Hammond

So Lovey, why can't we come together for the better good of our people and or, all humanity and shut this lie down? Covid-19

Look at the lies told on You and Mother Earth Lovey.

Look at life here on Earth.

You are there for me yes, but I need this petition therefore, I am coming to You Lovey, Mother Earth, the Universe, the Spiritual Realm, my true guides, and yes, Death. Death need to shut down their people now man come on now.

I do not have the power to command Death here on Earth Lovey. *At least I don't think so anymore.* However, I have you Lovey therefore, be my true hope and need including good and true voice.

*Mother Earth evil can be shut down in you including in the sky. You Mother Earth own vast territories; land space in you yet, humans are truly destroying you above and below. Why?*

*I need to plant more.*
*I need to live without fear.*
*I need to live without their Mark; vaccines of Death.*

I need to be self reliant on the Earth Mother Earth come on now.

I need to truly plant good.

Mother Earth, do you know the Pleasure and Beauty I feel just planting with Lovey.

No Mother Earth, why am I being denied my truth here on Earth?

Why do I not have my own peace of land where I can get up and be happy planting with God in you day in and day out?

No Mother Earth; what is so good about evil that evil have to dominate you Mother Earth?

Come on Mother Earth, there is pleasure in you.
There is beauty in you.

Am I the only one that sees this beauty, and can feel this beauty?

Aye Lovey, glory be to you, but I need.

I am needing on this day thus, I am needy.

Lovey, are you going to take away my beauty and pleasure from me?

Are you going to destroy my truth and true blessings with you?

I need this global petition Lovey.

I am not of Death but of Life. I need good and true life here on Earth Lovey come on now.

*Now tell me Lovey:*
WHY SHOULD I HAVE TO LIVE UNDER THE GOVERNMENTAL RULE OF WHITE MEN – THEIR MODERN-DAY SLAVERY?

My Life to Right is with you Lovey. So why are you allowing demons to take my Life and Right to Life from you?

Why should I live wrong and go to hell and burn?

*Why should I have to live to please the Devil or Death?*

*Why should I have to live to please Death's Children and People?*

Why create Earth then if you were going to allow the wicked and Evil to sabotage all life here on Earth Lovey?

You know what, let me go lay down and play my game because, I refuse the wicked and evil of life here on Earth Lovey and Mother Earth.

This is not acceptable for me or our good and true people. I so do not know what is the problem and why we cannot rid Earth of all Evil?

No, Evil is right away Lovey, why can't our goodness be right away?

Why worry about the Children and People of Death?

Let me stop because my anger is flaring, and I have to let it wain.


Michelle
August 2021

Tell me Lovey. Why is it that the Children and People of Life have to live amongst lawlessness?

Why is it, the Children and People of Life hath no say here on Earth?

Lovey, I complain to you a lot for the better good of life and I do blast you at times, but to what is happening now here on Earth; how is life worth it?

Fine Death have and has their people, but why is it that those who want and need true life here on Earth truly do not have it?

Why is it Life is a Sin here on Earth for the good and true and truly trying to be good?

No Lovey, I am not trying to stir your emotion this way and that way, all I need right now is for you to truly see my need and act genuinely, and truthfully on my need and needs. The passion I have for planting with you I truly need for you to keep yet, I feel as if my hands are not blessed. Maybe, no, I did not plant the wrong seeds with you Lovey, I planted the right ones, I am just not in the environment I need them to grow in. All is good though but Lovey, truly let this Covid-19 catastrophe end now. Truly let those who know the truth come out with the truth for the world populace to see.

*Lovey, I can't give up on you.*

*It is disheartening that I feel as if I am going to lose you here on Earth.*

*It is disheartening that more here on Earth isn't rallying for the truth and the true truth to be known.*

*It is disheartening that humans are forced to accept the white way.*

Lovey, the lie went as far as you and I've reminded you of this in other books. Now, I fear my value with you is naught.

I fear I do not have enough investment in you to conquer evil especially this Covid-19 Death Trap that is being forced on humans globally.

## WHERE IS THE TRUE VOICE FOR THE TRUTH HERE ON EARTH LOVEY?

I am in emotional pain and turmoil. No one should have the right to take you from me and those who truly need you.

Why isn't Mother Earth doing more to seal off all facets of evil in her, around her, in the sky above, and more?

Lovey, why do you not feel me and feel the preciousness of you in me?

Then Lovey, if you don't want or need to save anyone apart from me here on Earth, find a true spot to put me where we can grow good together. Yes, a place where we both can get beauty and pleasure out of planting with each other.

Lovey, I need segregation and separation for me and our good and true own here on Earth but you are truly not listening to me.

*I need that great divide where I have my own food, waterways that is independent of the food and waterways of the Wicked and Evil here on Earth.*

I need to be able to walk free.

Travel free.
Be free.

I truly do not need any war and strife Lovey come on now.

Now tell me Lovey, where is my beauty and true beauty in you?

Why leave me hopeless and tired in this way?

Where is your truth and true care?

Where is our gift of life together?

Where do You and I fit in here on Earth?

*I feel as if I am being massacred You Lovey Wise.*

Why?

Yes, I want and need to scream because you can't feel me or hear me in this way.

Let me go get dressed and take Queenie out because she is telling me her way that she needs her second walk.


Michelle
August 19, 2021

I am back Lovey. Queenie is done but I have to ask you this Lovey.

*If we as humans truly loved You, and truly loved Life, <u>would Earth be this way?</u>*

Would humans not be living to live instead of living to die? Would humans not truly invest in you truthfully?

Would humans not break away from lies? Would humans believe in lies when it comes to you?

I was thinking about Control Lovey.

Why do some live to Control?

## <u>IS IT NOT THE WEAK THAT SEEK CONTROL AND DOMINATION LOVEY?</u>

## <u>SO, WHY ARE HUMANS ALLOWING THE WEAK TO CONTROL THEM?</u>

*When I look at life Lovey, what does it profit anyone to seek control, and control here on Earth to go to hell and die?*

There is no good governance in Control Lovey come on now.

Maybe I am wrong, but for me, I just want to see people happy and living right.

As for my dreams, I am going to leave them alone because humans are unjust.

Dreams to do with Vybz Kartel, and my eldest son's ex girlfriend, and more I will leave alone.

Humans are the true Destroyers of Life.

Why say you want life yet, do naught to preserve your life here on Earth?

Why say you want life yet, destroy all life here on Earth?

*No Lovey,* **DUTTY CAANE CLEAN** *come on now.*

Look at how we as humans have and has destroyed Earth and each other.

*No Lovey, truly look at how some value* **MONEY OVER LIFE.**

Money cannot buy Life yet; you have many that kill for it; money without regard for their life, and the life of others.

Yes, I need Death to truly go with their wicked and evil own, but I need this going to be the right and just way Lovey come on now.

Different people and races have different gods Lovey yes, but what about true life?

Why do people walk away from life come on now?

What is so wrong about life?

And I've asked you this in other books Lovey come on now.

Yes, I am concerned and scared for life.

Yes, I wish humans globally would wake up and see the big picture, and make the necessary good changes for self, but I know many will not because; many are conditioned to think wrong and do wrong. Yes, it is sad, but this is the reality for billions.

Humans did turn Earth into a garbage heap; yes, their dumping ground literally.

Life do suck sometimes because good have to live amongst evil.

Good have to live amongst the unclean.
Good have to live amongst the unjust.

Good have to live amongst the dead in life here on Earth,

No Lovey. Why should Good surrender to Evil here on Earth?

Why should Good take on the ills of the Wicked and Evil?

I don't know but maybe one day you will find me good and true Lovey.

Maybe one day you will remember me true.

Michelle
August 19, 2021

Lovey and God let me write my perfect world with you. Let my truth touch every fabric of your being and truly help me.

As I seek your true help, truly be the one I need day in and day out.

Lovey, I truly want and need to plant more with you.

I truly need what we plant together to forever ever grow sweet, good, true, full of positive energy, ever healing, never dying, and more good and true things Lovey.

Together we must stay strong Lovey.

As for all my health issues and woes, truly write these health issues, financial woes, land woes out of my life and truly bless my hand, life, heath, truth, and more good and true things with you.

*Lovey in all I write in these books, let the words be blessed, received truthfully, heal, give more than hope, but truly bless the good and true who read these books, all who try to change for the better good due to the knowledge they find truthfully in these books.*

Lovey, in our land that we will reside in here on Earth, please keep all facets of negativity and evil away from our land and domain.

Lovey, we are together in truth therefore, no evil or negative energy including people must get access to our world and domain.

Lovey, impenetrable frameworks and foundations we must have continually more than forever ever without end.

Lovey, it's our new world and beginning so we must start right and true, be right and true, truly more than perfect for each other.

We must gather good and true strength from each other.

Oh Lovey, we have to be truly peaceful as well as, live in true peace. We cannot have any form of strife or fear in our land and lands. Therefore, Lovey, no creepy crawlers, insects, spiders, snakes, worms, bugs. No form of destructive anything we must have in our land and lands Lovey.

Lovey, Lovey, true beauty and positive energy we must have.

*An abundance of good food and clean water we must have all the time Lovey.*

*Our soil must be truly rich and fertile in everything that is good and true Lovey come on now.*

Lovey, we must continually have true Balance in our land and lands.

An abundance of clean water we must have at all times Lovey.

Lovey, our land and lands cannot be dirty.
All in our land and lands must protect and respect the environment; Mother Earth.

*We must work harmoniously with Mother Earth for everything we need water wise, food wise, clothing wise, planting wise, sleeping wise, temperature wise, and more good and true things.*

*Lovey, truly let the Moon work with us and shine positive and bright in our land.*

Lovey, you know I truly love to see the Moon at nights.

*Oh Lovey, please let Lone Star be in our land, and let Lone Star shine bright and true because; I do like to see Lone Star at nights as well.*

Lovey, Lovey, we have to plant roses; have our Rose Gardens, and our eatery by the river. Well, you know me and what I truly want and need to design for us by the river so that we can have breakfast, lunch, and dinner on our special days.

Lovey, Lovey, keep true to my heart and never ever fail me.

Lovey, be my true blessing and all that I ask of thee. Please let our will, I say our will because you are truly with me in my thoughts; well, all that I do good and true for you, us, and our good and true people.

*Lovey, truly write and take Death perfectly out of my heart and life, and out of the heart of our good and true own, and truly trying to be good.*

*Lovey, put in place the good environment you need us to be in. Truly let our environment and domain become a good and true reality for us here on Earth Lovey where we are segregated and separated truly and truthfully from everything that is wicked and evil no matter where on Earth, or anywhere the wicked and evil reside Lovey.*

Truly lock off all facets of evil from around me, inside me, in our domain, in our life here on Earth and in the Spiritual Realm, and more Lovey.

Lovey, no more pain and suffering ever for the good and true, you, me, Mother Earth, the truly trying to be good, and more Lovey.

*Strengthen us day by day Lovey so that when negative forces and people try to harm us, all they do fail and bounce back on that evil spirit, or person.*

Lovey, Lovey, truth we must have and live by all the time with you therefore, we must respect each other, respect you, have good moral values that we live by day by day.

*Lovey, Lovey, we must be knowledgeable. And whatever you do Lovey,* **never forget that YOU MUST BE OUR FIRST GO TO FOR EVERYTHING NO MATTER WHAT.**

No Lovey, to the true love and truth I have for you, I cannot leave this out. You must be our first choice and go to all the time. Even if it's to say Good Morning Lovey, have a blessed and true day.

Lovey, Lovey, true love always.

*In all we do Lovey, never let Mother Earth turn her goodness from us, and we must never turn our goodness from Mother Earth either.*

Lovey, we have to be of good courage right now.

Yes, I would like to come to you for all Black People but in truth, I cannot because not all Blacks are with you Lovey. I have to be real because you did warn me about Black People in my dreams as well as, you did show me them.

But however it is Lovey, truly shield me and our good and true from all that is to come. Let the exodus begin for us including me.

*In all we do to leave out of the land and lands we are in good and true Lovey, let none stop us, hurt us, try to set us up, kill us, and more.*

Lovey, let us have true passage out of the land and lands we are in.

Lovey, you know my passion and truth for everything when it comes to us and our good and true own.

*Lovey, all the wicked and evil do to eliminate us, let it be the wicked and evil that are eliminated.*

Lovey, no fighting or war must be in our land or lands. No Lovey, you have to be our true guide that guide and show us as well as, be with us day in and day out.

Lovey, we have to have a special day with each other where we just cook and sit and eat with each other.

Oh Lovey, we have to have an abundance of fruits.

Oh Lovey, fruit juice of different varieties we must have in our land and lands.

*Lovey, absolutely no Alcoholics thus, Alcohol we have to ban if you see that it will bring about drunkenness in our land and lands.*

Lovey, this is our new start therefore, absolutely no churches, or religion, no polygamy, no whoredom, no misuse of authority, absolutely no injustice. All must be fair and just Lovey come on now.

Aye Lovey good and true blessings always.

Lovey, in our lands we must never ever have health issues Lovey. All that we need to combat Heart Disease, Strokes, Cancer, Kidney Issues, Skin Problems, Infertility, any form of Depression, and more Lovey, we must have all the cures for them in our land and lands.

Lovey, we need knowledge therefore, I am coming to you for true and right knowledge.

Lovey, as your people, we cannot be fools anymore. Meaning, give you up for fools gold. Therefore, Lovey, Evil must never find us, they must be blind to us; cannot see us Lovey.

*Lovey, no form of evil can enter your domain Physically or Spiritually ever. I need this for us here on Earth where no Evil can enter our domain here on Earth ever Lovey.*

Life is truly not Death therefore, we need to truly live good and true, happy, clean, truly supportive, truly positive, ever growing up good and true.

*Lovey, we cannot lack knowledge.*
*We cannot live for control.*
*We cannot live to tear each other down.*
*We have to build each other good and true.*
*We have to be happy people that are blessed.*

Lovey, different people have different skills so let us live good with each other, and capitalize on the different skills to help our land and lands.

*Lovey, we can sell with our own in the different lands, but we must never ever try to outdo each other, cheat each other, nor can we over produce.*

The animals in our land and lands Lovey must be good and clean. As humans in our land and lands Lovey we have to think of the good and true animals that reside with us.

Lovey, no unclean animals or beasts we must have.

Lovey all the goodness I have not mentioned, let it all manifest here on Earth for our good and true people including me. My hope right now is that, people will find these books and let them truly take off without ever stopping.


Michelle
August 2021

Good evening Lovey, it's a new day for us. Had to go by my dad's and my last child came with me.

By your grace and mercy truly let me go over there on Monday returning Tuesday evening. I have to make sure things is right with him.

As for my dreams Lovey, age difference I did cover in other books. But Lovey, *many here on Earth truly do not care who they sleep with because they were not taught about Age Appropriation.*

Yes, it's wrong for a 50 year old to marry a 25 year old.

Age Appropriation is non-existent here on Earth because humans live by their wants and needs no matter if those wants, and needs are wrong.

*I also need to talk about YOUNG GIRLS MARRYING OLDER MEN AND PAWNING OFF CHILDREN THAT ARE NOT THEIRS; FOR THESE OLDER MEN ON THEM. This, the Spiritual Realm is reminding me of.*

*As for India.* Why am I seeing into this land Lovey?

Tell me Lovey, how can you have children and that child lock you up for you not to leave the home. This is the dream to do with India. I was outside this house by the gate and this Indian Girl in her twenties locked the gate with her mother inside. She would not let her mother out of the yard or home.

In the dream this was a regular occurrence. I could open the gate and I did. I opened the gate and went to where the elder Indian Woman was. She was by this tree, and you could see lady bugs on this tree in the backyard where the Elder Indian Woman was. Her daughter was not beside us and she was seeing the bugs on the tree. I believe I told them that part of the tree where the lady bugs were had to be cut down. The daughter agreed with me that; *the part where the lady bugs were had to be cut down.*

I am not going to analyze this dream as it's self explanatory.

I do not know if by the time I upload this book, there will be a bug infestation in India that affects trees and or, the food supply of India, Pakistan, Bangladesh, Canada, Indonesia, Southeast Asia, and more.

Therefore, the bugs – lady bugs I saw on the tree. I will go as far as sayings bedbug infestation. But, it was lady bugs on 1 tree that I saw.

## My other dream had to do with Me, Rihanna, Angela Lansbury, and Leonardo DiCaprio.

*We were sitting, and Angela Lansbury who was dressed in black was reading Rihanna's palm and I stuck my palm in there to be read. The opening of Rihanna's hand you could see countries. Madagascar, I remember. I am not sure if Africa was on her hand, but countries were outlined.*

Now with me sticking my hand out for Angela Lansbury to read my palm she said, *"nothing was there for me."*

After she said that, Leonardo DiCaprio paid off some bill, and Angela Lansbury paid 4 million dollars for a home.

I think Leonardo DiCaprio had 40 million dollars that's why he paid off this bill, and all of a sudden Angela Lansbury bought a house. I am not sure if England was where she bought the house.

So, from Barbados to England, I am not sure what is going to happen to these lands. I know for a fact without doubt Death own England, Barbados, and The United States of Death; America.

You know what, I am so not going to analyze this dream because; *I know Satan own the Entertainment Industry and certain Lands here on Earth.*

Satan owns the bank account of the different entertainers. This is nothing new for me. For many their soul means naught as long as they have money, feed death, do the work of demons, and more. So, this dream is self explanatory for me.

As for me having nothing. I do not have a piece of land where I can plant with God or even build homes for the good and true and truly trying that need homes.

I do not have the money therefore, when it comes to land and money here on Earth; *God and I truly do not have it* *THUS, ANGELA LANSBURY TELLING ME "NOTHING WAS THERE FOR ME."*

So yes, Satan owns many lands and bank accounts here on Earth literally thus, *Female White Death reminding me of this.*

And no, with me seeing Angela Lansbury in black, I do not know if she is going to die soon.

*Yes, black is death for me, but....never mind. I know how Death works and how Death teach me, and show me things here on Earth. So yes,* DEATH HAS AND HAVE AMASSED A LOT OF LAND HERE ON EARTH. THUS, DEATH CONTROL AND OWN THESE LANDS.

Michelle

There is so many things that is happening Lovey. You would figure humans would figure things out by now.

Sorry. Good morning Lovey as it's a new day, and it is hot outside.

Walked Queenie already and my daughter is in my bed sleeping. Her cousin has her bed well, sofa bed.

Body is sweating but that's okay. I truly do not mind sweating. Yes, I like to smell my sweat at times because the scent is different, and I am an odd person I would say.

While walking Queenie I was trying to connect with my inner being by doing navel/tummy rolls. It is difficult connecting to yourself. Now I am finding my navel is getting a bit sore, and it hurts. I so do not know why my navel area gets so sensitive.

As for my seeds Lovey, the first one is truly not fairing so well. I do not know if it's because I have my pot right at my window where direct sunlight is on my plant, but I am truly sad that one of our seeds in fading away, and I truly do not know what to do.

The sunlight is right. Maybe it's the soil and or, me giving our plant too much water. But Lovey, we did it. We grew plants from seeds. Yes, the process is slow, and I was a bit impatient because I wanted to see our seeds; all of them sprout within a week but it did not happen. You can't rush the planting process *__therefore, you cannot rush growth, or life.__* Everything hath time in life here on Earth. I just wished our first seed would have continued to grow instead of stopping you know. My other seed has sprouted lovely. And yes, I did only see one seed growing in my dream world. So, let's continue to grow good and true because I've started Ginger, Coconut, June Plum, Strawberries, and Apple. I don't think you wanted apple though.

But I am trying every little thing Lovey and I do hope all work best for us. Yes, I know you did not want Apple Seeds to be planted by me. Truly forgive me.

Oh man I wish I had a Car where I could go to the Farmers Market and get some Peas to dry and plant. I also need our vegetable garden Lovey. So, come 2022 by your grace and mercy, let me get a Car so that we can travel in style to get all we need to plant.

Lovey, you can't be Michelle Lazy now come on now. I need the right and true everything for us come on now.

Lovey I truly do not have the right soil.

I need Mother Earth.

I need to plant in the ground using the dirt and or, soil of Mother Earth.

I truly love planting with you Lovey, but Potting Soil is truly not for me; us.

For me, planting is truly not right – true if we are not planting with the soil; ground of Mother Earth.
We have our seeds growing and I am continuing the process, but I need the right land and soil for us.

*I need the soil of Mother Earth Lovey come on now.*

Now, as for my dreams, I truly do not know so, I am leaving them alone.

Let me think of you and only you.

Queenie is right by my side under the fan.

Would love to have breakfast with someone this morning but who. Now Lovey, would you like to go to breakfast with me?

It's a pity you do not have a Car or a Private Jet where you could jet me away to Los Angeles for breakfast, shopping, and back. Yes, all expenses paid by You Lovey. Yes, I know wishful thinking on my part as Los Angeles is burning, and Los Angeles is truly not clean.

Wow to the nastiness of that State.

And yes, my spur of the moment breakfast and shopping list with you Lovey.

Maybe we should start a *LIFE TO DO LIST WITH EACH OTHER LOVEY.*

The pleasure and beauty I find in planting with you Lovey; should be the same pleasure and beauty I find with you when it comes to having breakfast, lunch, dinner, and shopping with you. Yes, crazy me but; who would not want or need this beauty; crave this beauty?

Yes, it's unfortunate what we do for each other cannot add more life to our life here on Earth. Meaning, the pleasure and beauty I get from planting for you and with you Lovey, it's a shame that this pleasure and beauty can't add more good and true years to our life, heal our sickness and pain, keep us debt free financially and death wise, and more good, true, and beautiful things.

No, I don't want or need to think about the rest of the world.

I don't want or need control. All I need is life, true life, true beauty, true pleasure, true happiness, and more good and true things.

*Now Lovey, let me ask you this this morning.* <u>Why aren't more and more people seeing the truth of Covid-19?</u>

<u>This virus and all surrounding this virus and vaccine has and have to do with THE MARK OF THE BEAST AS STATED IN REVELATIONS OF THEIR SO-CALLED HOLY BIBLE?</u>

<u>Why aren't humans putting it together Lovey?</u>

<u>Death did fulfill their book.</u>

*All that Bob Marley told us in his songs has and hove come to pass, and Black People still have not figured it out.*

*Marcus Mosiah Garvey tried and failed.*

*We as Black People fail our self because we refuse to open our eyes to the truth.*

*I've failed because these books aren't known. Nor will Black People gravitate to the truth. Thus, Blacks are conditioned in Biblical; Religious Lies.*

Have humans become so blind that they cannot see anymore?

No, that was a stupid question Michelle. Humans have become that blind that they cannot see anymore.

Therefore Lovey, what is life then here on Earth apart from Death; the Death of Flesh and Spirit.

Christians claim they know you yet, are so blind; cannot see.

Muslims claim they know you yet, are so blind; cannot see.

Jews claim they know you yet, are so blind; are liars, thieves, murderers, falsifiers of all that is true and holy.

Catholics claim they know you yet, are so blind; are liars, child predators, thieves, falsifiers of all that is true and holy.

All denominations of religion claim they know God yet, are so blind; are liars.

*Now Lovey, if these people claim to know you, would they not see all?*

*Know all*
*Live by the truth*

*Would they not truly protect you from all that is going on?*

*Would they not step up with the truth globally?*

*Would they not protect your children and people from all the lies that are being told Lovey?*

*If all claim to know you Lovey.*
*Why is there so much Sin here on Earth?*

*Why is there so much War here on Earth?*

*Why do we hate each other so?*

*Why do we kill each other so?*

*Why do we destroy Earth, and do all to take all life from her; Earth?*

*Why do we destroy Life; our Spiritual and Physical Life with you Lovey?*

*Why do we do all that we do for a place in Hell?*

*Now tell me this morning Lovey.* **<u>WHY DOES THE LIFE OF ALL HUMANS HERE ON EARTH HAVE TO COME DOWN TO GREED, CONTROL, AND MONEY?</u>**

*Why can't humans globally see their life hath no worth or value to those who run the different countries of the world?*

*Why can't humans globally see their life hath no worth or value to the Pharmaceutical Greed; Demons of this world?*

*Why can't humans globally see their life hath no worth or value to the Corporate Greed; Demons of this world?*

*Why can't humans see them and realize their life hath no worth or value to self and others?*

*Humans kill everything in sight Lovey come on now.*

Look at how some hunt for sport. Meaning kill for sport.

**<u>WHAT VALUE HATH LIFE HERE ON EARTH LOVEY?</u>**

*Mother Earth.* <u>WHAT VALUE HATH LIFE IN YOU WHEN IT COMES TO HUMANS AND ALL THEY DO IN YOU DAY IN AND DAY OUT?</u>

<u>*Now let me ask all in humanity this:*</u>

WHAT IS LIFE TO YOU?

HOW DO YOU VALUE LIFE?

HOW DO YOU VALUE AND MEASURE THE LIFE OF OTHERS?

DO YOU EVEN THINK OF THE LIFE OF OTHERS?

*According to Death I have nothing. Is Death not truly correct; right?*

*What land and lands do I have here on Earth when it comes to truth Lovey?*

*What land and lands do I have here on Earth when it comes to truth in you Mother Earth?*

*Is all not taken by Death and the Children and People of Death?*

*Did Death not make their people rich here on Earth where some are untouchable?*

*Do Death's Children not make law and laws to protect their wicked and evil own thus, getting away with murder?*

*Do the Bible of Man; Men not justify the wrongs of Men; Humans?*

No Lovey, I hold nothing back from you. Please see with me.

Did the Bible of Man; Men not say you put enmity between the Children and People of Life and the Children and People of Death?

Is there not enmity in the hearts of the wicked and evil here on Earth Lovey?

*When you read the stories; lies of the so-called prophets, are they not governed by a different set of Law and Laws as compared to the average citizen?*

*In man's so-called Holy Bible, did prophets not break the Law and Laws of Life and get away with it?*

*Is this not the same thing that is continuing to; and or, is happen here on Earth?*

Are there not different Law and Laws set out for the Governments of the Globe, and the Citizens of the Land?

Governments get away with murder.

Governments get away with breaking every law set out for humans to follow.

Governments kill at will.

Now tell me Lovey, how is life just and fair here on Earth?

I petition you for the right and rights of the good and true and truly trying only, but nothing is being truly done by You and Mother Earth in my view.

How do we as your Children and People Lovey escape the Wrath of Death, and Deaths Children and People when we don't even have a boat to get to our land?

We don't even own any form of land here on Earth Lovey. Now tell me, where is our great and true escape, and escape route?

In all I see, I do not see many escaping. I see me escaping, but I do not see many or any with me.

*I did see me just me alone in our space Lovey therefore,* **WHERE DID OUR PEOPLE GO LOVEY?**

*Are you telling me;* **I AM THE ONLY ONE HERE ON EARTH THAT IS TRULY WITH YOU?**

*Are you telling me;* **I AM THE ONLY ONE HERE ON EARTH THAT WILL BE SAVED?**

*Are you telling me;* **I AM THE ONLY ONE HERE ON EARTH THAT IS TRUE TO LIFE PHYSICALLY AND SPIRITUALLY?**

Lovey, it makes no sense to me right now. How can people not want and need a better life not just for self here on Earth, but in the Spiritual Realm also?

I truly do not comprehend, overstand, or understand why humans truly do not think of their Spiritual Life.

There is a Life and Death to be had after the Spirit shed the Flesh. Why are humans not thinking about this aspect of their life Lovey?

It is a bit after 10am and I have not had breakfast yet.

So need to go lay down but can't because my daughter is sleeping in my bed.

Let me go make a cup of coffee because my tummy is getting a bit hungry.

Michelle
August 2021

So going to have cheese and crackers for breakfast.

I have no freedom in my room because my daughter is in my bed. I guess this is why I dreamt my nephew this morning. He was in my washroom, and I went into my washroom with him in there, and he kissed me on my cheek. He needed a toothbrush to brush his teeth and my daughter's makeup stuff was all over the counter as well as, on my toilet seat in my washroom. Plus, water; clear water was getting in one of the containers; floral basket like container. So, can't describe it proper for you. I also wanted to go to the washroom, but my daughter had her clear cosmetic makeup thingy on the toilet seat.

Have I been dreaming about kids lately?

Yes, especially twins.

So not going to worry because I truly do not know.

Man, sometimes I wish I had the money to hire a chef that can and would cook all my favourite foods. So, hate having to have to go into the kitchen to make breakfast.

My water should be boiling right now. So, I am going to go make my coffee. I have ripe bananas; I am going to have one and later I will see.

Michelle
August 21, 2021

*I am going to close off this book now Lovey because I truly do not want it to be too long. It's Monday August 23, 2021 and have mercy to what I see dream wise. However, I am not going to cry out for humans, nor will I cry out to You Lovey and Mother Earth to stop this. Humans has and have gone too far with their wickedness here on Earth. Mother Africa and Mother Earth have to do something positive for self now.*

The dream I had not too long ago had to do with Me and Meaghan Markle.

It was as if curved lines were in the Earth, and a Purple and Black Fan was being placed in the Earth; ground of the Earth.

I know what this dream means, and I will not stop the Destruction of Earth. There have to be; *must be a MAJOR CONTINENTAL SHIFT; DIVIDE.* This have to take place Lovey and I nor You Lovey must interfere. We cannot have compassion on humans because this destruction and divide hath to do with humans – the Sins and Different Sins of every human here on Earth.

*Mother Earth can no longer unify good and evil. Just as Evil is separated spiritually from Good, so must it be here on Earth. Good must be separated from all Evil here on Earth.*

Good must abide by life and the Law and Laws of Life.

I've pleaded with you for this separation; the Separation and Segregation of Good and Evil here on Earth. Good cannot die with the wicked and evil.

Good can no longer lay with and marry the wicked and evil.

*Mother Earth can no longer maintain and sustain any form of wickedness and evil.*

*Mother Earth have to; must comply with the Law and Laws of Life. Therefore, Deaths Children and People must go.*

Yes, I know Black People will not adhere to Life Lovey and they too; all Blacks that will not listen and unify truthfully to save self you must let go from now. They too cannot be saved because I am truly tired of the bullshit of Black People.

You cannot say you want life yet, *KILL YOUR LIFE AND ALL LIFE AROUND YOU.*

You cannot say you want life and, *LIVE WHITE – THE WHITE WAY.*

You cannot say you want life and, *DESTROY YOUR LIFE AND LAND.*

You cannot say you want life and, *DENY THE TRUTH OF LIFE INCLUDING DENYING YOU YOUR OWN BLACK GOD.*

You cannot say you want life yet, *REFUSE TO SAVE YOURSELF, YOUR FAMILY, AND MORE GOOD AND TRUE THINGS AND OR, PEOPLE.*

I've told you Lovey, no last-minute stragglers when it comes to Black People. I refuse all last-minute stragglers.

I will not back down from this Lovey come on now.

Black People are truly not with You therefore, you cannot be with them; those who refuse you, and truly refuse you due to their religious beliefs, generational lies, family lies, their religious upbringing, and more.

I can't be bothered with false hope Lovey. Meaning, I refuse to wait on people who are not ready.

You cannot buy time Lovey come on now.

So, why should I wait on people who are not ready?

No, I refuse to wait until they are ready. Don't drag yu foot; run.

Time is of the essence come on now.

It's time we Lovey prepare our good and true own and start the Exodus.

*So, with Meaghan Markle being of Jamaican American Descent, a British Royal, I know California, Jamaica, England is on the docket of Death destruction wise.*

*EVERY TECTONIC PLATE HERE ON EARTH INTERSECT THUS, THE LINES I SAW. Therefore, THERE IS GOING TO BE A MASSIVE CONTINENTAL SHIFT REAL SOON.*

I will not worry about this.

I will not worry about the lives of billions.

Nor will I worry about the Fault Lines of Earth; Mother Earth.

I will not pray for billions.

I will not petition you Lovey or Mother Earth for billions.

I categorically refuse to petition you Lovey and Mother Earth for the wicked and evil of Earth.

Life is precious to those who truly love life.

Life is precious to those who truly do not want or need to live with and amongst the wicked and evil of life.

The wicked and evil never thought of their life Lovey and Mother Earth so, why should life or any life including You Lovey and Mother Earth think of the wicked and evil?

Mother Earth must gather the good and true and truly trying to be good in one place if possible. It is these good people that Mother Earth, You Lovey, and Me should protect and ensure we have an abundance of clean drinking water and food. Therefore, Lovey, we have to start planting good and true so that when there is no water or food in many lands, we the good and true have as much water that we need, food that we need, health care that we need, healing fruits and plants that we need, and more good and true sustainable things. And yes, _we cannot share with wicked and evil lands. This must be forbidden._

_We cannot sell to wicked and evil lands; this must be forbidden also._

Evil never thought to preserve their life good and true, and the good and true cannot preserve their life and land for them; it is forbidden.

Death is their choice and because there is absolutely no water and food in Death's abode, none should be in the abode; lands of the wicked and evil here on Earth either.

_No Lovey, I have absolutely no compassion for the wicked and evil._

I've faced hell Lovey therefore, I know how far evil will go to maintain and sustain their evil ways here on Earth. Many people has and have died at the hands of the wicked and evil.

Many people trust Death for Life therefore Lovey, it is Death that must maintain and sustain their people. Life; You Lovey and Mother Earth cannot continue to give life by sustaining and maintaining the life of the wicked and evil here on Earth. As God and Mother Earth, you both have to step aside and let Death have their wicked and evil own. Therefore, I tell you Lovey:

_"CLOSE OFF THE BOOK OF LIFE NOW."_

_"LET THE JUDGEMENT BEGIN."_

**BLACK PEOPLE MUST BE HELD ACCOUNTABLE, AND BE JUDGED FOR THEIR EVILS AND DISOBEDIENCE.**

**BLACK LANDS MUST BE JUDGED DUE TO THE EVILS OF THEIR PEOPLE; BLACK PEOPLE.**

Therefore, Black Men, Black Women know you because, every thing; all your actions must now be fully and truly recorded if it has not been done.

**"BLACK LIFE MATTER."** *It is you as Black People that value not life.*

You and I Lovey have to be satisfied with who we have.

We have to be satisfied with those who have their name in the Book of Life.

We have to move on with life.

We have to move on with the truth and knowledge of life so that we can truly live and be happy.

## The greed of humans surpassed their need for good and true-life Lovey come on now.

Look at how humans have and has abused Mother Earth.

Look at the destruction of Earth by humans.

If humans had truly thought about life here on Earth, they would have preserved life here on Earth for the better good of self, life; all life that is good and true.

So, no Lovey, we cannot preserve life for Death. We have to; must preserve life for Good and True Life; the goodness and truth of our good and true own including those who are trying to be good.

If humans had wanted good and true life; You Lovey, they would not have chosen Death over Life.

*Humans would not be living to die. Humans would be living to live. So, yes, I am seeing more destruction and the Continental Sift that must happen, and I will not interfere. I more than categorically refuse to interfere.*

*Mother Earth must cleanse; purge herself of all the evil that is within her, and around her.*

Michelle

Yesterday my room was hotter than normal Lovey.

Wow to the heat.

It's a new day and my room is hot. Not even the Moon could cool me down last night.

Yes, no connection Lovey.

Why is it that the Moon evades me and my asking on certain nights Lovey?

It is so not fair that I am being denied my needs in certain ways.

Oh well Lovey, I am so not going to worry about it. I have you and truly hope that my name is beside yours and with you in the Book of Life.

No Lovey, I truly don't want or need to go to hell. I was so used to having my room cool and nice to now have hell; the fires of hell in my room. Yes, the heat that is in my room. It is unbearable Lovey come on now.

My back is important thus, I need cool breeze on my back to have hell consume me heat wise in my room yesterday and now this morning no. And no, I will not change my mind when it comes to the wicked and evil of life here on Earth.

Hell is not my home.

I cannot take the heat in my room therefore, I know for a fact without doubt I will not be able to take the Heat in Hell.

So nope, I more than categorically refuse Hell for Me, you Lovey, Mother Earth, our Saved, and the truly trying to be good.

I will not have any mercy or pity on them; the wicked and evil because; *LIFE IS TRULY WORTH LIVING.*

*I SHOULD NOT HAVE TO WANT TO GIVE UP LIFE DUE TO MY LIVING SITUATION HERE ON EARTH LOVEY COME ON NOW.*

The atrocities of the White Race has and have gone on for way too long. Yes, I am thinking about Mother Africa and how Whites have and has slaughtered Blacks.

Despite our sins Lovey, you know what; let me forget it because; *NOT ALL BLACKS ARE BLACK. SOME DO FALL UNDER THE WHITE BANNER OF DEATH.*

*And what Blacks fail to realize is:*

*WHEN YOU GIVE UP LIFE; YOUR LIFE WITH THE TRUE AND LIVING GOD, YOU GET DEATH. YOUR NAME MUST BE TAKEN OUT OF THE BOOK AND LIFE AND PUT INTO THE BOOK OF DEATH.*

**WHAT BLACK PEOPLE HAVE AND HAS FAILED TO RECOGNIZE, SEE, AND KNOW IS THAT; THE DEVIL HAVE AND HAS MADE**

## THEIR LANDS; BLACK LANDS RIDDLED IN SO MUCH SIN THAT YOU THE PEOPLE CANNOT PAY OFF YOUR DEBT TO DEATH. THUS, LAND AND PEOPLE OWE DEATH.

## YOU AS PEOPLE AND YOUR LAND CANNOT ESCAPE HELL AND DEATH.

As Blacks, we cannot say; we want God and continue to sever our ties with God.

God cannot help us if we continue to lie to Self and God.

God cannot help us if we continue to praise and worship as well as, live the White Way; Death's Way.

God cannot help us if our Good do not outweigh our Sins. Therefore, Black People; think and know.

Many Black Africans DID SEVER TIES WITH LIFE HENCE, DEATH PLAGUE AFRICANS AS AFRICA IS THE TRUE BIRTHPLACE OF DEATH.

As Black People, we fail to realize that when we accept Death in our life and lands; Death's Job is to destroy land and people. This is why many Black Lands are so poor despite having a plethora of resources.

All Blacks have, Death must take by any means necessary, and Death is taking. Thus, Black People Globally are truly not unified.

Thus, Death's Book; man's so-called HOLY BIBLE AND THE DIFFERENT RELIGIONS OF MEN.

*And I am going to truly leave off here Lovey because we both know the truth. We have to leave humans with their choice to die. You Lovey gave me seeds to plant over 100 million acres therefore, we can only save those who are true to you.*

We can only save those over 100 million seeds and acres. I cannot save the rest; those billions that belong to Death Lovey. I refuse to because; DEATH'S PEOPLE IS TRULY NOT TRUE TO LIFE, THEY ARE TRUE TO DEATH, and we have to leave them; Death's Children and People alone. This is the law, and we have to; must follow and adhere to the Law and Laws of Life.

*You did not tell humans to break the law Lovey. Humans listened to other humans and broke the Law and Laws of Life.*

*Humans were told:*

## *"THE WAGES (PAY) OF SIN IS DEATH."*

But humans did not listen.

Yes, none was told the penalty of one Sin.

*Yes, forgiveness is there from the person you erred; wronged, but there is no forgiveness of Sin when you knowingly and willingly break the Law and Laws of Life; God. Thus,* THE NEW BOOK OF KNOWLEDGE as written by Michelle and Lovey; God.

Beyond what I saw with Me and Meaghan Markle and or, before that dream, I was dreaming about going to Clarendon, Jamaica, and wanting fruits on my family's property but; there were no fruits. The trees were bare. Going further to where the family burial sight is, I saw mangos, and I called my last child to pick…no, I am getting this dream confused with another dream, I am sure of it.

Let me leave that alone. Suffice it to say, going back towards where my family's burial sight was, there was this huge flat screen tv not too far up in sky. I would say tree height was the height of the television that had a White Screen. The television was not turned on to a program. All there was was a White Screen with different selections on it. One selection I remember was Netflix. I am missing something. Before seeing the screen while looking for fruits, I turned to look back at the path I took, and I did see my dead step-grandfather coming towards me with his head down. He had meat on him and was of brown complexion.

That person I truly do not know who he is because, that is not what my dead step-grandfather looked like in the living. I can analyze this dream and so don't want to. Food Wise, I do not know what food shortage Jamaica is going to face because; *I know destruction is coming to that land.* *As for Netflix,* I am going to leave the death surrounding them; that organization and or, members and or, a member of that organization alone. *Netflix concerns me not right now.*

I've told you in other books, *Female Black Death own Jamaica.* So, however the destruction of Jamaica goes, this is truly up to Female Black Death. She truly do not have to sink the land of Jamaica. She can destroy it, but she does not have to sink the land. For me this is hard to explain because, somehow; *I think Black Female Death is preserving this land; why, I truly do not know.*

*Jamaica has and have been through so much yet, the people are truly not waking up. They would rather live death's way instead of living the right way.*

*No one is seeing for every death; murder committed on land by Jamaicans, it is more debt being racked up land wise and people wise.*

So yes, *BLACK PEOPLE DID TURN OVER SELF AND LAND TO DEATH.*

*BLACKS ARE DESTROYING BLACKS GLOBALLY.* Therefore, the Job of Death is done. Meaning, Death can just sit back and relax while humans kill humans for a place with Death in Hell.

*Thus, humans live the White Way; Death's Way instead of living Life's Way. Preserving and saving self from Death after the Spirit shed the Flesh.*

*So yes, in this way; the Job of Death is done.*

*Humans don't think.*
*Humans refuse to think.*
*Humans let others think for them.*
*Humans let others tell them what to do.*
*Humans let others lead them astray.*
*Yes, lead them to their death in hell.*

## *Why would you want to die to go to hell?*

*From another book. We cannot take the heat here on Earth now tell me; HOW IS YOUR SPIRIT GOING TO TAKE THE HEAT OF HELL?*

*How is your spirit going to survive hell when there is no water, food, or air conditioners in hell?*

*It's unbelievable how far humans especially BLACK PEOPLE HAVE AND HAS COME TO DIE.*

We talk about Slavery, but we are truly not free. Covid-19, and all the bullshit that humans are facing should be a true wake up call for humans to show them they are not free.

Humans are controlled.

Therefore, the Government and Corporate Greed do take all their rights; the rights and freedom of humans from them.

## DEVILS CANNOT LEAD.
## DEVILS CAN ONLY KILL.

And humans are dying literally.

BLACK PEOPLE HATH NO FREEDOM ANYWHERE HERE ON EARTH LOVEY COME ON NOW.

SO LONG AS WE LIVE IN LIES, BLACKS WILL NEVER EVER BE FREE COME ON NOW.

*Lies isn't freedom.*

Lies is death because lies are sins. Sins that shackle and chain you to death. Thus, humans truly do not know the cost associated with and or, to 1 Sin.

*Listen, you can say you live in a democratic country, I have freedom. And I will tell you this, read your constitution, and your constitutional rights because;* NONE IS FREE IN ANY LAND WHILST UNJUST LAW AND LAWS ARE INVOLVED.

## Therefore, the Constitution of Men only protect the evil and unjust.

*Freedom isn't biased.*
*Freedom isn't unfair.*
*Freedom is not this law or that law.*
*Freedom is not imprisonment.*

*Freedom do not take away your right to speak freely.*

*Freedom do not have this set of laws for this race and that race.*

*Freedom do not pit you against anyone or any race.*

*Freedom do not pit you against peoples' different religious beliefs.*

*Freedom do not imprison you for the herbs; healing plants God has given humans to help themselves here on Earth.*

*Freedom doesn't mean going into other peoples' lands with your self hate, greed, and massacre them for what truly belong to those people. See, Africa, North America, the Caribbean, European Blacks that was wiped out; the Black Plague and or, Purge, and more wicked and evil things done to Blacks and other Races.*

*Freedom isn't lying on God. See religion.*

*And yes,* **RELIGION IS THE BIGGEST PONZI SCHEME ON THE FACE OF THE PLANET THAT THE DIFFERENT THIEVES THAT RUN THE DIFFERENT CHURCHES GET AWAY WITH.** *Yes, get away with here on Earth but rest assured, absolutely none. Not one church goer, religious leader,* *and more can say their name is in the Book of Life because; all I have to do is show them their death;* <u>THE BOOK OF DEATH; MAN'S SO-CALLED HOLY BIBLE THAT THEY BELIEVE AND TRUST OVER THE TRUE AND LIVING GOD.</u> *Not one of you know that Religion pit you against God by taking your life physically and spiritually away from You and God. Thus, the different beliefs of the different religions globally.*

*Plus, I can show you the book;* <u>THE NEW BOOK OF KNOWLEDGE *as written by Michelle and Lovey; God.*</u>

*Plus, you have the entire catalog under the Michelle Jean banner of books that I can point to also.*

*Therefore,* <u>LIFE IS FREE. Death isn't.</u>

<u>Death come at a cost to all who have more Sin than Good.</u>

*Freedom isn't creating viruses and diseases to kill.*

*Freedom isn't designing and manufacturing guns to kill.*

*Freedom isn't giving people guns to kill each other; others.*

*Freedom isn't designing and manufacturing chemical weapons to kill.*

*Freedom isn't death.*

*Freedom is good and true life.*
*Freedom is truth.*

*Freedom is living right and doing right.*

*Freedom isn't red yie.*
*Freedom isn't grudgeful.*
*Freedom isn't control.*
*Freedom isn't greed.*
*Freedom isn't strife.*

*Therefore, humans really need to step back, look, reflect, and see where their life is headed.*

*Where they truly want and need to be.*
*What is important to them.*

*What is Life and Death to them, and more.*

*Michelle*
*August 2021*

I thought I was finished with this book, but I guess not.

It's August 24, 2021, and this dream is shaking me up right now because; I truly do not know what to make of it though, I know what it means.

Dreamt I went someplace; a gathering but I did not know what the gathering was for.

It was like I was in a backyard setting. Then I saw my ex-husband and wanted to leave, but I did not leave. I stayed.

Oh man someone was in a plaid – pink plaid shirt. I am not sure if it was him. He was now sitting down with a sad look on his face dressed in a black suit with the Holy Bible – Black Holy Bible in his hand. The Holy Bible was on the cover of the book, and it was encased in plastic wrapping. The book was brand new because he did not pull the wrapping off the bible. He was just holding the book as if lost; could not go on.

*Aye God. Allelujah*

*Glory Allelujah.*

*Judgement*

*Black Males are being more than judged.*

*Allelujah*

## THE BIBLE OF MAN IS THE JUDGEMENT FOR BLACK MEN INCLUDING SOME BLACK WOMAN. THEREFORE, YOU AS

# BLACK PEOPLE DO NOT KNOW THAT THE BIBLE OF MAN IS YOUR JUDGEMENT. BLACK PEOPLE ARE GOING TO BE JUDGED BY THE BIBLE AND YOUR BIBLICAL BELIEFS.

*Allelujah*

*Wow*

*Allelujah*

*Black People you are doomed if you truly do not unify truthfully.*

<u>See that gathering I was at in the backyard was a gathering after a funeral.</u> See, in the dream, his long-time girlfriend had passed away of Cancer, and they had just buried her. So, everyone met in the backyard.

*In the dream, I did not feel sorry for him, and I do not know if he felt I did not care but; he got up and left then came back.*

I was standing in the backyard, and I don't know what happened, but a garden was in the backyard, but you could not see the garden. All I know is, I was eating grapes. Grapes the size of jackfruit seeds if not bigger and sweet. I also wanted to plant the seeds of these grapes and some; about 1 or two I peeled.

Standing there eating my grapes this Basketball Player – American Basketball Player who acts sometimes. Let me check Google to see if I can find him. John Salley was standing beside me now. When I tell you John Salley clung to me, he clung to me. Did not want to leave my side and people picked up on this. It was as if he had his hand around my waist.

In the dream, John Salley picked up that my ex and I had had something going on, and he wanted to know what happed. So, we decided to go for a walk, but I realized I did not have my slippers on. I was bare feet and did not want to walk barefoot on the sidewalk least I get hurt; injured so, I decided to go inside the house for my sandals and he, John Salley was right there with me. Inside the home; house there was this light skinned young lady who gave John Salley money. They knew each other. I don't know if they were family, but she was smiling and quite nice.

So yes, I know what this dream means however, *I truly do not know what John Salley has to do with this dream.* But man was the grapes ever sweet. I just hope disappointment truly do not come my way.

So yes, I am going to have to find some grapes with seeds in them and plant them. It's weird. I was to go to my dad's house yesterday but did not get to go. Today is Tuesday and it's hot outside. Walked Queenie super early this morning and wanted to go for a walk by myself but, did not. Played my games then went back to sleep to have that dream and now I truly do not want to leave out of my apartment to go to my dad's house.

Every time I make plans to go to my dad's apartment, something comes along and say, no you are so not going. Your ass is staying home, and I truly do not know why.

Protection, yes, but man my body was drained a bit. You know when you can feel death, and death is draining you energy wise.

Yes, I can feel death; the sting of death. However, I will not worry about my ex husband and his situation because....let it go Michelle, let it go.

You have absolutely nothing to do with him therefore, let things go. God has and have been good to you therefore, <u>*GOD WILL ALWAYS PROTECT YOU.*</u>

Oh man, I have to call my family in the United States and see how they are doing.

I have to call Margaret also.

So yes, I am being protected all around.

*Man, I hope I don't meet no tall married man wanting to have a relationship with me. But really my Spirit World. I complained about you giving me a White Guy, now you have a married man – Black Married Man clinging to me. You know that is truly not right,* <u>*and adultery is a sin.*</u>

Therefore, no, I am so not going there this morning. I know Sin, and I refuse to Sin.

Oh man is it ever hard being single and in need sexually.

Lovey, why is this though?

When am I going to be allowed to have a partner Physically?

I am tired of it now come on now.

Why is it so hard for you to ordain the right person for me?

Yes, I know cleanliness but Lovey, how many people know about Life, the Law and Laws of Life What Constitutes Sin, the Penalties of Sin, and more?

So yes, Life Sucks for me on some days.

Why couldn't life be easy for me all the time?

No, life is easy for me because apart from my finances, land space, attitude of some of my children, health, my life is truly good. I have no other worries in this way. And my health issues back wise has and have tremendously improved to the point where I want and need to walk further in the mornings. So, shortly I am going to start walking far with myself. Yes, after I take Queenie home, I go for a proper walk with me and Lovey in the mornings now. I have to because I truly need to. I am connecting Spiritually Energy Wise to my body, and I have to continue to connect with me in this way as I am trying to heal myself – body Spiritually.

*You can heal your body Spiritually. You just need the plan and or, blueprint of how to do so.*

I do want breakfast, but I truly do not feel for eating anything right now. Yes, the hunger of my tummy has subsided from earlier this morning before I went back to sleep. You know what, I am only going to have a coffee because my body truly do not feel for food in that way.

Hopefully later I will get to go to my dad's house and come back tomorrow. If I don't go today, I will go early tomorrow, and come back the next day. We will see.

So, I am going to get a coffee; well, make coffee and see about the rest of the day. And please, do not think it creepy because I can see the death of people long before it happens.

*Michelle*

And to add a little bit more to this book as this is a *WAKING STATE VISION.*

I saw this Elder White Lady.

She was in the street on the right-hand side of the street going South. The area she was was by my dad's building.

She was walking on all fours; her hands and knees.

This vision I could not get away from because it happened twice. So, I truly do not know what is going to happen to Elder White People to cause them to revert on walking on their hands and knees in the street and or, road of Canada.

So, health wise, something is looming in Canada.

*I will not worry about this because Waking State Visions I truly cannot pinpoint. Nor will I worry about the Mental State of White People in Canada.*


Michelle
August 2021

## <u>*BOOKS WRITTEN BY MICHELLE JEAN 2021*</u>

*MY TALK JANUARY 2021*

*MY TALK JANUARY 2021 – BOOK TWO*

*MINI BOOK*

*JUST TALKING – THINKING*

*A LITTLE TALK WITH MOTHER EARTH*

*I NEED ANSWERS GOD*

*POETRY MY WAY*

*THE MIND AND SPIRITUALITY*

*I NEED ANSWERS GOD – PART TWO*

*MY NIGHTS*

*I NEED ANSWERS GOD – PART THREE*

*GOD IS GOOD*

*WHAT ABOUT US*

*WOW WHAT*

*AFRICAN – BLACK PEOPLE CUSS OUT*

*THE FIFTH WAVE – BLACK PEOPLE WARNING*

*FINAL CALL*

*JUST MY TALK 2021*

*THE TRAP*

*CHANGES*

*RACIST OR NOT*

*GIVE ME A REASON – SPIRITUAL CLEANSING*

*LIFE AFTER DEATH*

*THE DAYS LIFE SUCKS*

# <u>COMING SOON</u>
*DAY BY DAY*